DISCOVERING GOD'S HOUSE – WHERE GOD DESIRES TO LIVE WITH HIS PEOPLE ON EARTH

WRITTEN BY KEITH DORRICOTT

(PART ONE OF HIS BOOK: "ARE WE MISSING SOMETHING?")

PREFACE - SOME VITAL QUESTIONS

Is it possible for a Christian to be in the Body of Christ but not be in the house of God today? Is it possible for a church of Christians not to be a church of God? Is it possible for Christian worship to miss the mark? The purpose of this book is to examine and explore three implicit beliefs that are very prevalent in the evangelical Christian world today. These are:

1. That the **"house of God"** refers to all those living believers who, by virtue of having the Holy Spirit dwelling in them, are in the Body of Christ. Therefore all believers have the privilege of spiritual worship to God as a priesthood, wherever and however it may be offered.

2. That every local gathering of born-again believers in Christ is a "**church of God**" (as the Bible uses that term). They gather on the basis of all being members of the church "the Body of Christ" (sometimes referred to as "the true church"). Which particular church group they should gather with is largely a matter of personal preference.

3. That the **worship** of believers involves the presence of God coming down to men and women on Earth wherever they gather for that purpose.

The three main sections of this book deal separately with these three issues. They also attempt to show how these issues are related to each other in one integrated pattern of scriptural teaching. The first section deals with the topic of the house of God - what it is, what it does, and who are in it. It traces the concept of God living among a people on the Earth, from the first reference in Genesis, through Israel's experience of it throughout most of the Old Testament, and then to its replacement by the spiritual house of today as set out in the New Testament narrative of the Acts of the Apostles and in the epistles. What becomes apparent is how pervasive a subject it is, and how central it should be in the life and service of disciples of the Lord Jesus today. It is not by any means an incidental topic. God will also have a house in the future, but this book does not deal with either the Millennial temple or the eternal state on the new Earth, which are both subsequent aspects of this comprehensive purpose of God.

Section two deals with the topic of the churches of God, as the scriptural gathering of disciples in this age. It addresses questions such as:

- Why are there so many Christian churches today?
- Can we be true Christians without belonging to a church?
- Does it matter which church we attend?
- Are we fulfilling the "great commission"?
- Is the apostles' teaching relevant in the twenty-first century?
- Is the New Testament just first century history, or is it also a blueprint for us?

The third section addresses the subject of worship. It asks whether all worship is acceptable to God and what true worship involves. It explores the particular character of collective worship and addresses the question "Where does true worship take place?" It also considers what impediments there are to worship that can detract from the pleasure that God wants to get from it.

Before proceeding with these key issues, however, there are two topics that should be looked at first, because they underpin what follows. Examining them beforehand will give a proper perspective on the issues themselves. These topics are:

- the special relationship that we as believers in Christ have been eternally brought into as members of "the church which is Christ's Body" (chapter 1); and
- a brief historical perspective of the development of the Christian faith throughout the centuries, which has led to our fragmented twenty-first century Christian world (chapter 2).

This book is offered to all true believers in the Lord Jesus Christ who are serious about their lives and service for Him, and who welcome opportunities to explore ways in which they may be able to please Him more. In the pages that follow, as we delve into the highly relevant and inter-connected issues of God's house, God's church, and true worship, which are at the heart of the life and service expected of every disciple of the Lord Jesus, we shall have to keep in mind the cardinal principle that the Reformers used - "sola scriptura" – "by the Scriptures alone". The Scriptures, the written Word of God, will have to be the test of everything that we seek to discover. And then, as one Bible teacher put it, "If you show me what is in that book, you put me under an obligation to do it."

INTRODUCTION

CHAPTER ONE: THE CHURCH THAT CHRIST IS BUILDING

"The church, which is His body, the fullness of Him who fills all in all." (Ephesians 1:22,23)

When Christ told His apostles one day in Caesarea Philippi that *"upon this rock I will build My church"* (Matthew 16:18), He was announcing something totally new. Although it would be based on the eternal fact of His deity, as confessed by Peter, this church had not yet been brought into existence. The word "church" as used in the Bible does not have the same meaning as it is often given today, which is a physical building used for religious purposes. The word church in the New Testament is a translation of the Greek word *"ekklesia,"* from which we get our English word "ecclesiastical." It means people who have been called out to be together, a distinct assembly or congregation. Thus, when the Lord said that He would build His church, He was referring to people, and it was to be spiritual, not physical.

Old Testament clues

Various clues had been given about this church in the Old Testament, but never before had it been referred to explicitly. Later the apostle Paul would describe it as *"the mystery of Christ"* (Ephesians 3:4). What was this mystery and what were some of these pointers that had been given previously?

First of all, for instance, when God created the first man, Adam, He provided Eve as a wife for him (Genesis 2:21 - 25). However, she was also a picture of this future company of believers who would become Christ's eternal companion, an illustration of the church the Body of Christ. Eve had been taken from Adam's side while he was in a deep sleep, just as this church is the result of Christ's deep ordeal at Calvary. Another picture that is given is that of Asenath, who was the Gentile bride that Joseph had been given while he was in Egypt (Genesis 41:45). Joseph was heir to the promises that God had given to his great-grandfather Abraham. On the other hand, Asenath was a Gentile, an Egyptian woman, and so she did not have the same heritage. Yet she was given to Joseph to share his life and inheritance. Similarly the church the Body of Christ is not restricted to Jews, but is inclusive of all nationalities.

Although it had been hinted at back in Old Testament times, this church did not exist at that time. It did not apply to Israel as God's chosen people on Earth. It was something new that began when the present age began, after Christ's exaltation to heaven, on that day of Pentecost when the Holy Spirit was poured out (Acts 2:1-4). It required that the Gentiles be included so that it might be universal.

Building this church

The details of this church that Christ is building were revealed first to the apostles, including the apostle Paul who provided most of its teaching in Scripture, and through them to all the saints (Ephesians 3:2,5; Colossians 1:26). It was an all-inclusive message: all believers regardless of culture or background were equal members of this church, called "the church which is His body" (Ephesians 1:22). Each believer in Christ was then, and is now, built into it by being baptized by Christ in the Holy Spirit. Today this invisible spiritual baptism takes place simultaneously with the believer's new birth: *"By one Spirit were we all baptized into one body, whether Jews or Greeks, whether slaves or free; and were all made to drink of one Spirit"* (1 Corinthians 12:13).

(The original Greek shows that the baptism is "in" the Spirit. It is not the Holy Spirit who does the baptizing, but Christ Himself – see John 1:33.) Once believers are in this church, they cannot ever be put out of it or leave it. Their place in it is permanent. It is eternal and the Body itself is indestructible. Each believer is an indispensable member of it, like a part of a human body, and each member is intended to have an important part in its on-going strengthening (Ephesians 4:16). We are told that Christ Himself cares for this church and preserves "her", because one day she will be united with Him as His bride (Revelation 19:7):

"Christ also loved the church and gave Himself up for her, so that He might sanctify her, having cleansed her by the washing of water with the word, that He might present to Himself the church in all her glory, having no spot or wrinkle or any such thing; but that she would be holy and blameless" (Ephesians 5:25-27).

This church began at Pentecost. Believers will continue to be added to it until the Lord returns to the air for her, at which time she will be complete and intact. Those believers who have died will be raised; those still alive will be changed, and together - as one church - they will meet Him in the air (1 Thessalonians 4:16,17). And so the first time that Christ will meet His church bodily will be when He comes to the air for her. That is why the dead in Christ cannot go to meet Him ahead of those who are alive at His coming. He will meet her intact, as His bride - all believers together at once. That is what He is looking forward to.

The apostle Paul told the Ephesians that, when Christ returned to heaven, God His Father: *"put all things in subjection under His feet, and gave Him as head over all things to the church, which is His body, the fullness of Him who fills all in all"* (Ephesians 1:22,23). This tells us that this church, which would consist of all believers in Him from Pentecost on, is intended to be His "fullness," to magnify the glory of Christ, by being His complement. This will reach its culmination in the future, when all believers are perfectly united with Him and there is no created being outside His active authority.

Building up the Body

Meanwhile Christ continues to build up His church, by feeding her, caring for her, and holding her together, as believers hold fast to Him as Head: *"no one ever hated his own flesh, but nourishes and cherishes it, just as Christ also does the church"* (Ephesians 5:29); *"...holding fast to the head, from whom the entire body, being supplied and held together by the joints and ligaments, grows with a growth which is from God"* (Colossians 2:19).

He takes personal responsibility for her. He does this through the work of the Holy Spirit, whom He has sent to indwell all believers, as He explained to His apostles on the night before Calvary:

"I will ask the Father, and He will give you another Helper, that He may be with you forever; that is the Spirit of truth...He abides with you and will be in you."

"The Helper, the Holy Spirit, whom the Father will send in My name, He will teach you all things, and bring to your remembrance all that I said to you."

"The Spirit of truth who proceeds from the Father, He will testify about Me."

"When He, the Spirit of truth, comes, He will guide you into all the truth; for He will not speak on His own initiative, but whatever He hears, He will speak; and He will disclose to you what is to come. He will glorify Me, for He will take of Mine and will disclose it to you."

(John 14:16,17,26; 15:26; 16:13,14)

Christ said that the believers who would come after Him would multiply the works of God that He had been doing in His life on Earth: *"I say to you, he who believes in Me, the works that I do, he will do also; and greater works than these he will do; because I go to My Father"* (John 14:12).

What should members of the Body aspire to?

It is the Lord's desire that the character and unity of this Body be reflected by all living members on Earth. For this to be accomplished, all these members must be fully linked together and be under the direct control of the Head, Christ Himself. Just as a human body cannot function properly if any part is missing, dislocated, or damaged, or if there is any blockage to the brain, so it is with the functioning of this spiritual Body. If there is any disunity or any disconnection from the Head, or any underdevelopment of any part, then the display on Earth of the nature of the relationship into which believers have been brought will be impaired. That is why Christ prayed to His Father on His last night: *"I do not ask on behalf of these alone, but for those also who believe in Me through their word; that they may all be one; even as You, Father, are in Me and I in You, that they also may be in Us, so that the world may believe that You sent Me"* (John 17:20,21).

Not only would the behaviour of individual believers be impaired, but so would the fulfillment of the Lord's desire for believers to be together in unity. Paul went on to tell the Ephesians what this building up of the Body was intended to result in. He expressed it this way: *"until we all attain to the unity of the faith, and of the knowledge of the Son of God, to a mature man, to the measure of the stature which belongs to the fullness of Christ"* (Ephesians 4:13).

In other words, full maturity of believers together will mean that they express the divine unity which characterizes the church which is His Body. This is not just describing the personal spiritual growth of each of us as individual Christians. It is describing the full coordinated development of such believers joined in divine testimony. He described it as the result of each individual member doing its proper part, being equipped spiritually to do so, and being fully joined together with the other parts:

"He gave some as apostles, and some as prophets, and some as evangelists, and some as pastors and teachers, for the equipping of the saints for the work of service, to the building up of the body of Christ...but speaking the truth in love, we are to grow up in all aspects into Him who is the head, even Christ, from whom the whole body, being fitted and held together by what every joint supplies, according to the proper working of each individual part, causes the growth of the body for the building up of itself in love" (Ephesians 4:11,12,15,16).

Paul said that we are to not be like children, but we are to become mature. (In 1 Corinthians 14:20 he elaborated on this by referring to being *"children in understanding."*) As long as we as believers together are lacking in our understanding and in our devoted adherence to all the teaching that Christ has given us to carry out (which is described as *"the faith"*), we will not experience our full relationship with Him. We will limit His work for us today as He lives and serves in the presence of God (the unity of *"the knowledge of the Son of God"*), to progress to this goal of expressing the full relationship implied in the figure of His Body. Paul warned the Colossians about the possibility of falling short of this when he wrote: *"Not holding fast to the head, from whom the entire body, being supplied and held together by the joints and ligaments, grows with a growth which is from God"* (Colossians 2:19).

He was talking to them about indulging in worldly things or wrong teaching and practices. In verse 16 he had said, *"Don't let anyone judge you."* We are not to be influenced or led astray by any teaching, example, or criticism of others, no matter how convincing it may be. We are to keep pressing on towards the goal together.

It is about relationships

This imagery of a body is all about our relationships - with Christ as our Head, and with each other as members. The Body, with its different but inter-dependent parts, is all under the control of the Head. The supply of everything it needs in order to grow up and mature as one united person all comes from Him, but it flows to them through each other (Ephesians 4:15,16). (This interdependence is illustrated in Ephesians 5:22–33 by marriage between a man and a woman, which is the earliest and most intimate of all human relationships. The ideal in marriage is for the couple to achieve a relationship where each partner is so united with the other that they behave as one.) But there is a lot more in the New Testament that applies to us as Christians than the teaching about the church which is Christ's Body, as wonderful as that is.

When the apostles wanted to provide teaching on how disciples should gather together, how they should serve God, and how they should deal with problems such as sin and disobedience, they did not use the imagery of the Body. Those are things that are dealt with in the teaching about churches of God and the kingdom of God, which are not identical to the church the Body, but are intended to depict it. For example, no person can ever be put away from the Body of Christ; his or her position in it is absolute, unlike their position in a local church of God, which can change. Also there is no reference to admonishing or disciplining other members of the Body, but there are such references to those in churches of God (Romans 15:14; 1 Thessalonians 5:14). The reason for this is that the church the Body is blameless and perfect (Ephesians 5:25-27), and this is what saints and assemblies on Earth should aspire to.

Fellowship within the Body

While all believers are members of the one Body and therefore do have an invisible spiritual connection with each other "in Christ" (Romans 12:5), in practice there can be limits to the fellowship they should have with each other. Paul shows that the Body can only function and be built up as it receives what it needs from Christ, and as it ministers those things to its members: *"...and not holding fast to the head, from whom the entire body, being supplied and held together by the joints and ligaments, grows with a growth which is from God" (Colossians 2:19).*

As a result, not all sharing that takes place among believers can automatically be assumed to be the fellowship of the Body. We are each responsible to hold fast to the Head by engaging only in teaching and service that is according to Christ and not to things that are of human origin (Colossians 2:20-23). This means that we each have to learn from Scripture to tell the difference. And so there can be limits in practice to the degree to which Christians may feel free to join in fellowship with others (1 Timothy 1:5).

Understanding this fundamental and unique teaching from Scripture about the church the Body of Christ is important for us as we begin this study of what the Scriptures teach about the three issues of God's house, God's church, and true worship. In this way we can properly relate it to, and distinguish it from, other things. Why is it that this inherent spiritual unity among those who are "in Christ" is not evident today to a greater extent? Why are there so many divisions among Christians? For the answer to these questions, we will have to go back in history to understand how the Christian world developed to the state that it is in today. That is the subject of our next chapter.

CHAPTER TWO: HOW WE GOT TO WHERE WE ARE TODAY

"I know that after my departure savage wolves will come in among you, not sparing the flock." (Acts 20:29)

The twenty-first century Christian world is very different from what it was in the first century. Unlike then, today there is a multitude of Christian churches, denominations, sects, and groupings. There is also a seemingly endless variety of "doctrines" and practices among them. These days a disciple of the Lord Jesus has to search for the truth of God. And it is not always obvious where to find it. To understand how the present state of affairs came about, let us quickly trace the development of the Christian faith through the centuries, with particular attention on the teaching of the Lord to His apostles that was to be passed down.

The forty days

After His resurrection, the Lord Jesus spent forty days with His eleven apostles. He was preparing them to carry on His work after His departure. During that time, *"He had by the Holy Spirit given orders to the apostles whom He had chosen. To these He also presented Himself alive after His suffering, by many convincing proofs, appearing to them over a period of forty days and speaking of the things concerning the kingdom of God"* (Acts 1:2,3).

The culmination of that instruction was what is often referred to as the "Great Commission": *"Jesus came up and spoke to them, saying, 'All authority has been given to Me in heaven and on earth. Go therefore and make disciples of all the nations, baptizing them in the name of the Father and the Son and the Holy Spirit, teaching them to observe all that I commanded you; and lo, I am with you always, even to the end of the age'"* (Matthew 28:18–20).

We are not told the details of what He taught them during those forty days, but we can deduce it very clearly from what they did after He left, as recorded for us in the Acts of the Apostles and the epistles.

Pentecost

After the Lord had left His apostles and ascended to heaven, they and His other followers waited together in Jerusalem, as He had told them to. When the Day of Pentecost arrived, the Holy Spirit descended on them all, and Peter preached the first gospel sermon of the new era to those who came to investigate. The result was that about three thousand of them believed, were baptized, and were added together to those already there. And so there came into existence at the same time two vitally significant but different entities that would continue in parallel - the church the Body of Christ, consisting of all believers in Christ, having been baptized in the Holy Spirit (Acts 2:38) (which we looked at in the previous chapter), and the church of God in Jerusalem (see Acts 8:3 and Galatians 1:13), consisting of all baptized disciples who would continue consistently in what they were being taught.

What they were being taught became known as "the apostles' teaching" (or "apostles' doctrine," Acts 2:42). The apostles taught it, but what they taught were the commands that they had originally received from the Lord, which later became known as "the faith" (Acts 6:7). This church in Jerusalem continued to grow, until persecution from the Jews forced most of them to leave the city. Other churches of God sprang up in the towns and cities where they went. These churches were all founded on the same teaching, and they stayed linked with each other. They were a community, which later was referred to as *"the fellowship of His Son, Jesus Christ our Lord"* (1 Corinthians 1:9 NKJV). This unity of teaching and fellowship was maintained initially by the apostles and other prophets, primarily by their visits (e.g. Acts 8:14; 11:22) and writings.

But gradually other elders were appointed in the churches (first mentioned in Acts 11:30) to oversee them and to care for the saints in them. The New Testament records that by the end of the first century the work had spread throughout the eastern and northern Mediterranean areas of the Roman Empire, and it names many individual such churches of God.

The end of the apostolic period

By the end of the first century, all the apostles had died. They could not be replaced by others because a requirement to be an apostle of the Lord Jesus was that a man must have seen Him in resurrection and have been personally commissioned by Him. The foundation teaching that the apostles had laid down in every place was complete by this time. It was, as Jude described it, *"the faith which was once for all handed down to the saints"* (Jude verse 3). However, as the years went by, many of these fundamental teachings began to be lost, and the churches increasingly allowed error and human tradition to come in. This inevitably brought divisions among them. The apostle Paul had seen this coming. In his epistles to Timothy, he wrote:

- *"The Spirit explicitly says that in later times some will fall away from the faith"* (1 Timothy 4:1).
- *"The time will come when they will not endure sound doctrine; but wanting to have their ears tickled, they will accumulate for themselves teachers in accordance to their own desires, and will turn away their ears from the truth and will turn aside to myths."* (2 Timothy 4:3,4)

For example, the church in Ephesus to which Paul had previously written an epistle (Ephesians 1:1) was in danger of having its divine lamp stand removed (Revelation 2:5); that is, God would no longer have recognized it as one of His churches. In that epistle, Paul had been able to dwell at length on the marvellous truth of the church which is the Body of Christ (as we looked at in the last chapter), but by this time the saints needed to be warned that they had left their first love and needed to repent.

Deepening decline

The deterioration continued and the Scriptures became practically unavailable to most people, many of whom were illiterate, and they were eventually banned from public use in many places. Some of the developments that eroded the teaching of the Lord were as follows:

- By the second century, baptism came to be regarded as necessary for salvation. Later immersion was replaced by sprinkling, and then infants began to be sprinkled in the hope of ensuring their salvation.

- Around the same time, a trend was emerging whereby clergy were being appointed, distinct from the congregations, headed by a "president" (presiding bishop) in each church, taking over the leadership and all active service. The people were told that they could not serve God without these men as priests.

- As early as the second century, a variety of holy days and mandatory days of fasting was introduced and legislated.

- In the third century, the concept was introduced (later called "purgatory") of an intermediate destination of the souls of the dead. These souls, it was taught, could only be released to heaven by payment of money and by prayers to dead saints. This eventually led to the idolatrous worship of Mary the mother of Jesus.

- By the fourth century, the simple remembrance of the Lord Jesus in the bread and wine was replaced by a sacrificial "mass," in which the bread and wine were considered to be "trans-substantiated" into the actual body and blood of the Lord (although this term was not used until later).

- In the fourth century, the adoption of the Christian religion by the emperor Constantine brought about the union of church and state, and the doctrines of the church were formalized at the Council of Nicea.

It declared, among other things, that eternal salvation was only available by keeping a number of "sacraments" (such as baptism, confirmation, the Eucharist, and penance).

- This was followed by a split between the Roman church in the west, and the orthodox churches in the east. In the Roman church, the Bible began to be withheld from everyone other than the clergy. It was generally only available in Latin, which very few people could read. Other books came to be regarded as of equal or greater authority, and the hierarchy of the church set itself up as the sole interpreter of the Bible.

- Subsequently, indulgences to atone for wrongdoing began to be sold (sometimes in advance) to raise funds for building basilicas and for other church purposes.

- In the sixth century, the position of pope ("father") was established as the leader of the Roman church. By the twelfth century popes were being established as heads of state, and in the nineteenth century the pope came to be considered as infallible.

Rediscovering the light

In the midst of all this darkness and error, it was the Protestant Reformation in Europe in the fourteenth to sixteenth centuries that largely began to reverse the decline. Beginning with godly men such as John Wycliffe, Martin Luther, and William Tyndale, the essential truth of salvation by the grace of God, by faith alone, was rediscovered. The Reformers' motto was "*sola scriptura*" - "by the Scriptures alone." They rejected the church's claim to be solely entitled to interpret Scripture and to modify its teaching in the light of experience. They studied the Scriptures for themselves. Wycliffe, Tyndale and others began making Bibles available. Wycliffe stated: "The knowledge of the revealed will of God is to be found alone in the Scriptures." The invention of the printing press by Johan Gutenberg in 1454 made possible more widespread distribution of Bibles and accelerated this process.

In the centuries that followed, more and more of the fundamentals of the apostles' original teaching were uncovered, as the Word of God became increasingly the subject of enlightened study by Christians. Valuable truths emerged, such as those pertaining to the church the Body of Christ, disciples' baptism, the Lord's Supper, and the importance of evangelism and good works. Gradually these truths began to be put into practice in place of the wrong teachings and practices that were so entrenched. It is always the case that, when the truth of God is discovered from the Word of God and is then applied, things begin to change.

It was in many ways similar to what had happened late in Israel's history, when the book of the law was found after it had been missing for many years. This was the book in which Moses had written the commandments of the Lord at Sinai centuries before. Hilkiah the priest found it in the house of the Lord, which was in disuse and disarray at that time, and it led to the reforms that King Josiah initiated:

"Then Hilkiah the high priest said...'I have found the book of the law in the house of the LORD.' And Hilkiah gave the book to Shaphan who read it...And Shaphan read it in the presence of the king...When the king heard the words of the book of the law, he tore his clothes...The king went up to the house of the LORD and all the men of Judah and all the inhabitants of Jerusalem with him, and the priests and the prophets and all the people, both small and great; and he read in their hearing all the words of the book of the covenant which was found in the house of the LORD. The king stood by the pillar and made a covenant before the LORD, to walk after the LORD, and to keep His commandments and His testimonies and His statutes with all his heart and all his soul, to carry out the words of this covenant that were written in this book. And all the people entered into the covenant" (2 Kings 22:8–11; 2 Kings 23:2,3).

However, as a general rule, as truth was rediscovered from the Bible it was not widely embraced. There tended to be resistance to any such change and new teaching. Just as today, it was hard to distinguish between what was true scriptural teaching and what was human tradition, and it was even harder to reach agreement and to institute changes as a result of new scriptural revelation. It therefore usually required those who held a conviction about such truth to break away from existing churches in order to put into practice what they had learned. Inevitably this process was slow and not at all peaceful.

That is why the Christian world today is so fragmented. That is why there is such a variety of denominations, with so many different versions of "the truth" and differing views on the relevance of certain aspects of the Lord's teaching.

Unfinished business

However, in all this marvellous recovery, some key aspects remained hidden to many Christians. These included God's continuing desire to have a collective people gathered on Earth that He could call His own and live among - an identifiable people who were living holy and obedient lives in unity with one another. This unity, not achieved by compromise, but by reaching a common and proper understanding of, and subjection to, the complete revealed truth of God, has been elusive over the years, and yet it is vital. To some Christians, the present diversity of belief and practice among believers appears not to give cause for concern. Rejoicing in the fact of us being *"all one in Christ Jesus"* (Galatians 3:28), as we do, they appear never to have seen what God intends for us beyond that. Surely if we miss that, we are missing much - and so is the Lord.

As we saw previously, on the last night of His life the Lord Jesus prayed for this unity of those who would believe on Him through what the apostles would teach:

"I do not ask on behalf of these alone, but for those also who believe in Me through their word; that they may all be one; even as You, Father, are in Me and I in You, that they also may be in Us, so that the world may believe that You sent Me. The glory which You have given Me I have given to them, that they may be one, just as We are one; I in them and You in Me, that they may be perfected in unity, so that the world may know that You sent Me, and loved them, even as You have loved Me" (John 17:20–23).

His prayer, *"that they all may be one,"* was not a reference to their unity as members of the Body of Christ. That spiritual unity is guaranteed and cannot be lost. He did not need to pray for that. He was praying that believers would all be united in their service and lives for Him - that they might all truly be "one." And yet that certainly is not the case today. The unity of the Body of Christ is not seen in practice amongst believers today. Expressing that unity remains unfinished business of the highest priority.

The path to unity

What then is the key to achieving this unity that Christ prayed for? Is it for us to disregard our differences of views and just all get along with each other? No - surely it is much, much more than that. It is nothing less than having a united understanding and adherence to all that the Lord taught His apostles and that they then taught to others. It involves putting it into practice in an actual fellowship, *"the fellowship of God's Son"* (1 Corinthians 1:9 NKJV). This requires that we understand from Scripture all that He has commanded us, as the Great Commission states.

If this goal is to be achieved to any degree today, it has to begin with us having a proper and shared understanding of the Word of God, and how it applies to us today. Any accord has to be based firmly on what the Scriptures actually say and mean in order to be *"the unity of the Spirit"* (Ephesians 4:3). The Holy Spirit will not lead us into anything that is contrary to His Word. The Lord Jesus said that one of the reasons the Spirit would be given would be to lead us into the truth (John 16:13).

CHAPTER THREE: SOMETHING MORE THAN THE BODY

"You also, as living stones, are being built up as a spiritual house." (1 Peter 2:5)

"One thing I have asked from the LORD, that I shall seek: that I may dwell in the house of the LORD all the days of my life, to behold the beauty of the LORD and to meditate in His temple." (Psalm 27:4)

When David wrote these words in Psalm 27 he was expressing his deep and chief desire to dwell where God dwells. He certainly was not talking about just going to church. He was talking about where he was most at home, where he wanted to spend his time, and with whom he wanted to spend it. As a man after God's own heart (1 Samuel 13:14) David wanted God's house to be the focal point of his life. Yet David did not have the opportunity to experience it the way that we can today, as disciples of the Lord Jesus Christ. It would take the future death, resurrection, and exaltation of Christ to make that possible. But we can only experience such dwelling by God with us if we first realize what the house of God is, and that it is in fact a possibility for us.

Why did David want so much to live where God lived? It was because he knew that this was where he would come to know God the best. He knew it would allow him to have the closest and most lasting relationship with the Lord. We see people at their fullest when we see them where they live. As David said in the previous Psalm, *"O LORD, I love the habitation of Your house and the place where Your glory dwells"* (Psalm 26:8).

What was it that David longed to see about God that we might miss? What is God really like in heaven? We are told that He lives in unapproachable light and brightness (1 Timothy 6:16), that there is total joy in His presence (Psalm 16:11), and that His will is always entirely carried out there (Matthew 6:10). Further, God's unlimited power and authority are seen as He directs the activities of the countless mighty angels that surround His throne, as they cover their faces and execute His every command (Psalm 103:20). From there, too, God's kindness and love are seen in His full provision for all His creatures (Acts 14:17), and above all in His salvation for mankind (which is only partly seen on Earth).

These (and more) are aspects of Almighty God that are also in view where He dwells on Earth. David knew that, while we can see glimpses of them from outside His house, in order to see them more fully we have to come inside. Nevertheless he knew that all the days of his earthly life he could only experience God in His dwelling place on Earth, which was but a copy and a shadow of the true tabernacle in the heavens (Hebrews 8:5; 9:23).

Where does God live today?

The concept of the eternal God living with people in a "house" on Earth may seem strange. Even Solomon posed the question, *"Will God indeed dwell with mankind on the earth? Behold, heaven and the highest heaven cannot contain You"* (2 Chronicles 6:18). The subject of God living in a "house" on Earth among a people of His own is not one we hear a lot about today. And yet it is a subject that runs from Genesis to Revelation. When someone refers these days to "the house of God," more often than not they are talking about a church or a synagogue or a temple of some sort - a building, a "place of worship" where people can go for religious activity. But that is not what the Bible means when it uses that expression. Happily, there is much in Scripture which not only tells us of the reality of God dwelling on Earth, but also of how it is possible for us to be part of it.

Has God ever lived on Earth?

The Old Testament is full of references to God's house. It began with the dream that Jacob had at Bethel (with the famous "Jacob's ladder" that is sung about). It continued through the Israelites' construction of the tabernacle in the wilderness, then Solomon's great temple in Jerusalem and its partial restoration later under the leadership of Ezra. And then when Christ came to Earth about four centuries later, the temple, then rebuilt by Herod, was still the centre of Israel's religious life.

It continued that way, despite God having deserted it (Matthew 23:38; 27:51), until the temple was destroyed by the Romans in AD 70. But by that time the Christian era was in full swing. The disciples of Christ who gathered together in service did not have a central site, and church buildings were not a feature of their activity. In fact, they sometimes had to meet in secret because of persecution. Those early disciples often met in small groups in homes or in public places. It was only after the Roman Emperor Constantine converted to Christianity in the early fourth century that Christians began to build large, impressive cathedrals and other places of worship. But did any of these constitute God's house? Did God reside in those buildings? Was that where people had to go to be in His presence?

Is the church the Body the house of God?

Many believers today have some understanding of what the church the Body of Christ is. It is a uniquely New Testament truth. There often seems to be an assumption, however, that other things which are called "of God," such as "the kingdom of God," the "church of God," and the "house of God," are synonyms for the Body of Christ, and therefore everything that we are told about them automatically applies to all living believers.

However if, as we have been seeing, there is not presently a unity among believers alive today on the Earth, what is the basis on which we can all claim to be part of any of these other things? Can God live in a divided house? Does He have a divided kingdom? We need to explore whether there is in fact something missing in this explanation, that there is something additional that God wants us to put into practice today, something distinct from the wonderful reality of being members of the church which is Christ's Body.

Are our bodies the house of God?

When a person puts faith in Christ for salvation, we are told that the Holy Spirit of God takes up permanent residence in their body, making it a "temple" (1 Corinthians 6:19), a place where God resides. The Lord Jesus had promised His apostles on the night before His death that the Spirit of God, who to that point had been "with" them, would soon be "in" them (John 14:17). He was referring to what would begin on the day of Pentecost, when the Holy Spirit would be poured out on them, and they would be baptized in the Holy Spirit. This was going to be a very new and fundamentally different experience for them and for all believers.

The Lord had previously spoken about this when He was in Jerusalem at the feast of tabernacles. He had called out to those who were busily engaged in the temple grounds on the final day of the feast: *"If anyone is thirsty, let him come to me and drink. He who believes in Me, as the Scripture said, 'From his innermost being will flow rivers of living water.' But this He spoke of the Spirit, whom those who believed in Him were to receive; for the Spirit was not yet given, because Jesus was not yet glorified"* (John 7:37-39).

It would require the glorification of Christ in heaven after His resurrection to make possible this wonderful provision of the Spirit of God to permanently dwell in all those who would put their faith in Christ. As the apostle Paul later explained: *"Do you not know that your body is a temple of the Holy Spirit, who is in you, whom you have from God?"* (1 Corinthians 6:19). The Spirit has been given to us in order to be a guarantee of our eternal salvation (Ephesians 1:13), to lead us as disciples in our transformation as sons of God into likeness to Christ (Romans 8:14), and also to be the power source of our service for Him (Acts 1:8).

Christ had referred to His own physical body as being a temple when He said to the Jews, *"Destroy this temple, and in three days I will raise it up"* (John 2:19). They had thought He was referring to Herod's great temple in Jerusalem, and they reacted strongly against His statement. They used it in their accusations against Him at His trial, misquoting Him in the process. But He was speaking about His own impending death and resurrection. He was talking about His own body being a temple, so making the first reference to the human body as a temple. For every believer in Christ today the same thing is wonderfully true - that their body is a temple of the Holy Spirit; God Himself lives within them. But is that what puts them in God's house? Or is there something else?

Are we in God's house today?

What did the apostle Paul mean by *"You are a temple of God"* (1 Corinthians 3:16) and *"We are the temple of the living God"* (2 Corinthians 6:16)? What did the apostle Peter mean by saying *"you...are being built up as a spiritual house"*? (1 Peter 2:5) What did the writer of the epistle to the Hebrews mean by *"we have a great priest over the house of God"* (Hebrews 10:21) and *"whose house we are, if we hold fast..."* (Hebrews 3:6)?

Unlike the wonderful truth of the church the Body of Christ, this subject of the house of God is not something that is confined to the present Christian New Testament age, even though the house that exists today is different from what existed previously. It is a subject that begins right back in the book of Genesis and pervades most of Scripture. It was central to the experience of the people of Israel with God in the Old Testament, it continues for us in the present, and it will do so in the future. There are many lessons about it from Israel's past that can really help us to understand how it applies to us today, and so we will examine those next.

CHAPTER FOUR: GOD'S HOUSE IN THE PAST

"'What kind of house will you build for Me?' says the LORD, 'or what place is there for my repose?' Was it not My hand that made all these things?'" (Acts 7:49,50)

While God has only had one house on Earth at any one time, throughout the centuries it has taken different forms in successive periods. Like so many other subjects in Scripture it begins in Genesis where Jacob's revelation plants many of the seeds of what would be revealed later. While he was on his journey from home, Jacob stopped at a place called Luz, just north of modern Jerusalem. While he slept he had a dream in which God showed Himself and confirmed to him the covenant that He had previously made with his grandfather Abraham and his father Isaac. In his dream, Jacob saw a ladder set up on the Earth that reached into heaven, with the Lord at the top. When he woke up he said, *"How awesome is this place! This is none other than the house of God, and this is the gate of heaven"* (Genesis 28:17).

And so he named the place Bethel, meaning "the house of God." There was no building or other sign of habitation there. But Jacob had learned that the key thing about God's house is not what man builds. Rather it is that God chooses a place to dwell in, and it is His presence in that unique spot on Earth that makes that place God's house. To mark it he set up as a pillar the stone that he had been sleeping on, and later he returned to live there. This was God's first indication that He had a dwelling place on Earth in which He was prepared to company with men.

The revelation of the house of God in Genesis has a second part, whereby God required Jacob and his household to dwell with Him at Bethel: "*God said to Jacob, 'Arise, go up to Bethel and live there, and make an altar there to God'*" (Genesis 35:1). An altar was to be built and from that time forward, in God's dealings with His chosen people, the altar was irrevocably associated with the house of God. Those that dwelt there, in God's house, correspondingly had to be purified and to change their habits. Jacob renamed it "*El-Beth-el,*" "the God of the house of God," because he saw God there, which is the whole point of God's house. Previously God had been referred to as "*the God of Abraham, Isaac, and Jacob,*" the God of individuals, but this was something more.

The tabernacle in the wilderness

About five hundred years later, Jacob's descendants, the people of Israel, accepted God's covenant at Mount Sinai that established them as His people. They were to be uniquely His holy nation, distinct among all the peoples of the Earth, and to be a kingdom of priests (Exodus 19:6). Then God said to them through Moses, "*Let them construct a sanctuary for Me, that I may dwell among them*" (Exodus 25:8).

And so, on Mount Sinai, He gave Moses detailed instructions for the construction of a tent (or tabernacle, meaning a dwelling place) and all its furnishings. The God of heaven was going to live among them in a tent, just as they were living in tents. The tabernacle itself was made of ten identical linen curtains. They had to be joined in a certain way, so that it would be a single covering (Exodus 26:7). When it had been finished completely in accordance with the pattern Moses had been given, the visible glory of the Lord came down and filled it (Exodus 40:35). It then became the centre of the camp of Israel during their time in the wilderness, as well as afterwards when they crossed into the land of Canaan.

Later Moses, when he was thinking about the unique privilege of God living among them, exclaimed to the people, *"What great nation is there that has a god so near to it as is the LORD our God whenever we call on Him? Or what great nation is there that has statutes and judgements as righteous as this whole law which I am setting before you today?"* (Deuteronomy 4:7,8). It is important to realize what had led to this honour being given to Israel. They had been chosen by God, redeemed from Egypt by the blood of Passover lambs, "baptized" in the Red Sea (1 Corinthians 10:2), and then brought to Sinai. There they pledged their obedience, saying, *"All that the Lord has spoken we will do"* (Exodus 19:8). On that basis they were given the covenant and given the privilege of contributing materials to the construction of God's house on Earth. They did the work, but it was God's design to the last detail. Once it was completed, God's presence filled it and its service could begin. To them and to no other nation had been given *"the service of God"* (Romans 9:4 NKJV).

This tabernacle was not a creative invention by Moses. It was patterned after and served as a picture of *"the true tabernacle"* that exists in heaven, *"which the Lord pitched, not man"* (Hebrews 8:2; see also Hebrews 9:24). It affected where the various tribes camped; it affected the arrangement in which they travelled; and it affected their daily and annual schedule of activities. It introduced a divine order into their lives, which had not existed before. Having God living among them made all the difference. The tabernacle was where they met with Him; it was their *"tent of meeting"* (Exodus 40:2).

Israel alone was the people of God on the Earth, even though they were insignificant in other peoples' eyes, as merely a nondescript nomadic collection of ex-slaves without a land of their own. However Balaam, a foreign prophet who was allowed to observe them in their divine order as they camped in the plains of Moab, described them as they truly were: *"Behold, a people who dwells apart, and will not be reckoned among the nations"* (Numbers 23:9).

Soon afterwards, in his great closing speech to the whole congregation of the people who would finally go into the land (but without him), Moses said: *"You are a holy people to the LORD your God; the LORD your God has chosen you to be a people for His own possession out of all the peoples who are on the face of the earth. The LORD did not set His love on you nor choose you because you were more in number than any of the peoples, for you were the fewest of all peoples, but because the LORD loved you and kept the oath which He swore to your forefathers, the LORD brought you out by a mighty hand and redeemed you from the house of slavery, from the hand of Pharaoh king of Egypt"* (Deuteronomy 7:6-8).

Also the people were instructed that, when they did enter the land, they were not to offer and worship in just any place that they chose. God had designated a place within that land where He was to be worshipped: *"Be careful that you do not offer your burnt offerings in every cultic place you see, but in the place which the LORD chooses"* (Deuteronomy 12:13,14).

And so Israel uniquely had been given the privilege of the service of God, which was centred on the house where God lived among them. What an honour they had, but it brought with it certain obligations: of living holy lives (Psalm 93:5), of obeying the law of God, and of carrying out the many ordinances of divine service (Hebrews 9:1). God was now living among them, which made them distinct from every other group or nation of people on the Earth at that time (Isaiah 43:1-7).

The centerpiece of the tabernacle was the Ark of the Covenant, in the most holy place. Above it dwelt the presence of God among His people. God called it His "strength" and His "glory" (Psalm 78:61). When Israel occupied their promised land of Canaan, the tabernacle stopped its journeying and was placed in Shiloh, just north of Bethel (Joshua 18:1). However under King Saul, the Ark was taken away into battle against the Philistines, where it was captured. Then God *"abandoned the dwelling place at Shiloh, the tent which He had pitched among men"* (Psalm 78:60). The ark did not return to Jerusalem until years later, when David became king of all twelve tribes. Meanwhile the tabernacle itself (without the Ark) moved about to Nob, to Gibeon, and finally to Jerusalem.

The temple of Solomon

Five hundred years after Sinai, when King David wanted to replace the tabernacle with a more permanent and suitable structure, a temple, he was told that he would not build it, but that his son Solomon would do so. And so David prepared and stockpiled supplies for it. Just as Moses had, he received the instructions for it from God Himself (1 Chronicles 28:19). The only item that was carried over from the tabernacle was the Ark of the Covenant.

After David's death, his son Solomon did build the house for God. God had appeared to David on the summit of Mount Zion, the mountain of the Lord, the same place where Abraham had previously taken Isaac to offer him. David offered a sacrifice there, and God answered it by fire from heaven. When David saw this he said, "*This is the house of the Lord*" (1 Chronicles 22:1). He knew that this was the location that God had chosen for His temple to be built (2 Chronicles 3:1).

It was a glorious temple. Once again, when it was finished, the glory of the Lord filled it and the people knew that God's presence was among them. Again it was the focal point of Israel as a nation. It was on the site that God Himself had designated in the holy city of Jerusalem, on Mount Zion, in the land of Israel's inheritance. Israel's full worship and service to God, their daily offerings and annual feasts, all centered on God's house, the temple. When it was finished, the Lord appeared to Solomon and said, *"I have chosen and consecrated this house that My name may be there forever, and My eyes and My heart will be there perpetually"* (2 Chronicles 7:16). God had put His name on His own house.

The psalms

The psalmists frequently expressed what it meant to them to have this privilege of God living among them:

- *"How blessed is the one whom You choose and bring near to You to dwell in Your courts. We will be satisfied with the goodness of Your house, your holy temple"* (Psalm 65:4, written by David).
- *"Zeal for Your house has consumed me"* (Psalm 69:9). This is the Scripture that the Lord's disciples recalled when they saw Him angrily driving out the moneychangers from the temple courts (John 2:17).
- *"How blessed are those who dwell in Your house! They are ever praising You"* (Psalm 84:4). This is a psalm of "ascents," sung as the people were going up to Jerusalem to the temple for the annual feasts.
- *"I was glad when they said to me, Let us go to the house of the LORD"* (Psalm 122:1). This psalm of David is also a psalm of ascents.

The second temple

Several generations after Solomon, however, the great temple was destroyed by the Babylonians. God allowed this to happen because of the nation's continued disobedience. Its divine service came to a halt. The people were deported into captivity in Babylon. They were deprived of their collective service in the house of God. However godly individuals could continue to live devoted lives in their alien environment, as we see with both Ezekiel and Daniel, who prophesied during this period of exile.

Finally, after seventy years, permission was given for the exiles to return to Jerusalem. Every one of them had a choice to make: would they go? Most of the people had been born in Babylon and life was comfortable there. Why uproot themselves and go to a land they did not know? There was only one valid reason to go - Jerusalem was the place of the Name. God's house was there, lying in ruins. Only a small remnant did go, just over forty thousand of them (Ezra 2), but they went with happy hearts: *"Then our mouth was filled with laughter, and our tongue with joyful shouting"* (Psalm 126:2). Ezra the scribe and Zerubbabel the governor led them. Willingly they began reconstruction of the altar and the temple, but opposition from their enemies put a halt to the work for several more years until, at the urging of the prophets Haggai and Zechariah, the work was resumed. As God told the people through Haggai: *"Go up to the mountains, bring wood and rebuild the temple, that I may be pleased with it and be glorified"* (Haggai 1:8). Finally the temple was completed and its divine service recommenced (Ezra 6:14-18).

The structure was far less impressive than Solomon's temple had been, and it would have been tempting to dismiss it as being insignificant. It was made of inferior materials, and it did not have God's visible glory hovering over it. But it was still the house of God, and God accepted the service that was offered there, even though it was offered by just a remnant of His chosen people. He said that He still took pleasure in it. It was the obedience of their hearts that He valued. To dwell again among a people who loved Him sufficiently to obey His Word was something very precious to God – and to them, *"the sons of Israel, the priests, the Levites and the rest of the exiles, celebrated the dedication of this house of God with joy"* (Ezra 6:16).

The third temple

Finally this second temple was itself replaced under King Herod, with a structure that took forty-six years to build (John 2:20). This was the building that was in Jerusalem at the time the Lord Jesus was born. When He came to Earth in His humanity, as expected He frequented the temple. It was His Father's house, the house of God, and it was the focal point of the life and service of Israel. And so He did. He was brought there firstly by His parents, at forty days of age, as the law required (Leviticus 12). At age twelve he came back with them for the Passover feast (Luke 2:42), but then stayed behind. When they found Him He told them that He had to be *"in My Father's house"* (Luke 2:49). Even as a young boy He knew that He should be there to learn, prior to Him beginning His public ministry.

At the age of about thirty, as He began His ministry, Jesus came back to the temple and found that it had become very commercialized. Travellers needing to buy animals for sacrifice were being taken advantage of. This infuriated Him and He drove out the moneychangers in his zeal for God's house (John 2:13–17). Later, because the leaders of the Jewish nation in Jerusalem had rejected Him, He announced that "their" house was left to them desolate. It was no longer going to be God's house. God was no longer going to be living among His people Israel: *"Jerusalem, Jerusalem, who kills the prophets and stones those who are sent to her! How often I wanted to gather your children together, the way a hen gathers her chicks under her wings, and you were unwilling. Behold, your house is being left to you desolate! For I say to you, from now on you will not see Me until you say, 'Blessed is he who comes in the name of the Lord!'"* (Matthew 23:37-39) They had refused to let Him draw them to Himself, and so in their rejection of Him they lost the privilege of divine service. However, things were about to change.

God wants to be at rest

After God had created the heavens and the Earth in six days, He rested on the seventh day. In doing so He established the unit of time of one week, which has been a mainstay of the working life of men and women. God's purpose in creation was that He might enjoy His creatures and have fellowship with them, that He might be appreciated and worshipped by them. Then sin came in to make this impossible without the work of redemption. Christ had to take on humanity and give His life to redeem us back to God. But this work of redemption has been accomplished, and so God is now bringing to completion His great eternal purpose. His work of creation is complete, and Christ's work, which He came to do on Earth, is also complete.

And so now God wants to enjoy His rest - not a rest if relaxation or inactivity but the full enjoyment and fellowship with the people that He created and has redeemed. That is what God means when He talks about His "rest." God's house is where He wants to be at rest with them: *"'What kind of house will you build for me?' says the Lord, 'or what place is there for my repose?'"* (Acts 7:49)

When Israel was in the wilderness at Kadesh-Barnea on the verge of entering their promised land, they refused to go in. God was furious with them, because that was the place of His intended rest with them, and they were depriving Him of it: *"I was angry with this generation...as I swore in My wrath, 'They shall not enter My rest'"* (Hebrews 3:10,11). He waited for the next generation, and they went in instead. Even then it was not God's final rest; there was something more to come: *"If Joshua had given them rest, He would not have spoken of another day after that. So there remains a Sabbath rest for the people of God...let us be diligent to enter that rest, so that no one will fall, through following the same example of disobedience"* (Hebrews 4:8–12). The same diligent obedience is required of us if we would enter God's rest today, a rest which (as we shall see) is still associated with the house of God.

Does God need a building?

None of the buildings that served as God's house throughout the Old Testament were His final place of rest. As Stephen said to the Jewish Council: *"The Most High does not dwell in houses made by human hands; as the prophet says: 'heaven is my throne, and earth is the footstool of my feet; what kind of house will you build for me?' says the Lord, 'or what place is there for my repose? Was it not my hand which made all these things?'"* (Acts 7:48–50).

Clearly, all these structures, from the tabernacle to Herod's temple, were just temporary, just physical representations of the spiritual reality. God Himself lives in heaven in the tabernacle not made with hands (Hebrews 9:11), where no human eye of ours can see, *"The Lord is in His holy temple; the Lord's throne is in heaven"* (Psalm 11:4). However, it has always been God's great purpose to bridge the gap between Earth and heaven. That was the significance of the ladder that Jacob saw. Jacob realized that God's house on Earth is also the gate of heaven, the means of accessing God where He is. It was for this reason that Jesus the Son of God came to this Earth in human form. It was not only so that we, poor sinful human beings, could have access to heaven one day through salvation, but also that the redeemed could access heaven collectively. This is not just in the future; it is for us today. Christ wanted to make it possible for us to serve His God and Father spiritually in God's immediate presence in heaven during our lifetimes. He wanted God's dwelling place to be not only in heaven or on Earth, but for the two to be linked.

It was for this purpose that the Holy Spirit was given. From the time of creation (Genesis 1:2) it has been the work of the Spirit to bring about on Earth what God the Father in heaven wishes to be done. And so the tabernacle and all the temples that followed it were just temporary, physical replicas; the true sanctuary in heaven is spiritual, for God is spirit (John 4:24). Those physical structures serve as a parable for the present time (Hebrews 9:9). God's house on Earth today is a spiritual house, and we will look at that next.

CHAPTER FIVE: THE HOUSE OF GOD TODAY

"You also, as living stones, are being built up as a spiritual house."
(1 Peter 2:5)

Peter wrote his first epistle to encourage disciples who were living in several provinces of the Roman Empire, and through them to us now. Being part of a Jewish dispersion, as believers they were also "aliens" who were being persecuted for their beliefs. He wrote to them:

"You have been born again not of seed which is perishable but imperishable, that is, through the living and enduring word of God...Therefore, putting aside all malice and all deceit and hypocrisy and envy and all slander, like newborn babies, long for the pure milk of the word, so that by it you may grow in respect to salvation, if you have tasted the kindness of the Lord... And coming to Him as to a living stone which has been rejected by men, but is choice and precious in the sight of God, you also, as living stones, are being built up as a spiritual house for a holy priesthood, to offer up spiritual sacrifices acceptable to God through Jesus Christ" (1 Peter 1:23–2:5).

Being born again

He reminded them that their salvation experience had involved them being "born again" into a new life, not produced by something that could perish or expire, but by the eternal Word of God. Possessing this eternal life, they could never lose it.

It was guaranteed by the Holy Spirit (Ephesians 1:13) and was in God's hands, not theirs (John 10:28,29). Just as God's Word cannot be destroyed, neither can the life that it imparts. Therefore they were able to be certain that their salvation was permanent. At this point they also had the indwelling Holy Spirit and were members of the Body of Christ. Did this make their spiritual experience complete? Far from it - it was just beginning, as he proceeded to tell them.

Growing as a disciple

He then referred to their growth through continually taking in the Word of God as disciples. They were growing up in their salvation in the same way they had originally received it, by drinking in more and more of the pure milk of the Word of God, the way a newborn child does. Putting this Word into practice involved them putting away sinful behaviour that belonged to their old nature. They could not have done that without the Holy Spirit being within them. They were disciples, but where would this discipleship lead them?

Being built into God's house

He then described how they became part of the spiritual house that God was building. They must come to Christ as their Lord - not just coming to Him once in a single occurrence, as they had done at salvation. (The form of the word "coming" in the original shows that it is repetitive.) They must come in on-going response of obedience to His claims on them. They were being built up with others as a spiritual house. They were being brought into line with Christ as the corner stone. The purpose of that house was to be a holy priesthood, to engage in priestly service as a people entirely for God. And the nature of that holy priesthood service was their offering up of sacrifices which were spiritual in nature, not physical, which God would accept, as they were presented through Jesus Christ.

Living stones

Peter was showing them, and us, that the house of God is no longer a physical place, or a structure. It is made up of people, "living stones", stones made alive by the Word of God and ready to be built into place. Christ Himself is described here as a living stone, as an "alive man," and so are we as His disciples.

Christ had been rejected by the Jewish leaders when He was on the Earth. He did not fit into what they were building, and so they discarded Him the way a builder would discard a stone that was unsuitable. He Himself had quoted this Scripture from Psalm 118:22: *"Jesus said to them, 'Did you never read in the Scriptures, 'The stone which the builders rejected, this became the chief corner stone; this came about from the Lord, and it is marvelous in our eyes'?'"* (Matthew 21:42).

But God had taken Him, that stone discarded on Earth, to be the supremely precious and uniquely chosen "stone," and had placed Him in heaven as the very foundation stone, the "corner stone," of that spiritual house that He was going to build. Peter further quoted Isaiah 28:16 from the Old Testament, *"Therefore thus says the Lord GOD, 'Behold, I am laying in Zion a stone, a tested stone, a costly cornerstone for the foundation, firmly placed. He who believes in it will not be disturbed.'"*

These Scriptures, dating from hundreds of years before Christ, show that God had revealed His plan well in advance. He had revealed that there would be a spiritual house, with its corner stone laid in heaven, in which people would engage in spiritual service to God, based on their on-going faithfulness to Jesus Christ as Lord. It was Jesus' death, resurrection, and ascension to heaven that made this great plan possible. The New Testament Scriptures that deal with the house of God today refer to it in two general ways. They address it as being a place to live and also as a building structure. Let's look at both of these concepts.

The house as a place to live

To the church of God in Corinth, Paul wrote, *"Do you not know that you are a temple of God and that the Spirit of God dwells in you? If any man destroys the temple of God, God will destroy him, for the temple of God is holy, and that is what you are"* (1 Corinthians 3:16,17). He also wrote to them, *"We are the temple of the living God; just as God said, 'I will dwell in them and walk among them; and I will be their God, and they shall be my people. Therefore, come out from their midst and be separate, says the Lord and do not touch what is unclean; and I will welcome you'"* (2 Corinthians 6:16,17).

Here the apostle uses the term "temple," because a temple of God is a place where God dwells. Paul is showing the house as a place for God, not just to visit, but to stay - a "dwelling place" (habitation) for God on Earth among believers who are identified as His people. It is therefore a holy place. This necessarily requires that those people among whom God is staying live holy lives and be separate from ungodly things. God lives among them in the person of the Holy Spirit, who is the person of the godhead who makes the presence of God a reality on Earth in this age. This dwelling of the Holy Spirit is in addition to His indwelling of each believer's individual body, as Paul describes in 1 Corinthians 6:19. And so the temple itself is indwelt by the Spirit of God, as Paul also stated in his epistle to the Ephesians, *"In whom the whole building, being fitted together, is growing into a holy temple in the Lord, in whom you also are being built together into a dwelling of God in the Spirit"* (Ephesians 2:21,22).

In addition, the apostle wrote to Timothy about proper conduct in the house of God, *"I write so that you will know how one ought to conduct himself in the household of God, which is the church of the living God, the pillar and support of the truth"* (1 Timothy 3:15). The word for "household" in this verse is the same word as "house" used elsewhere, but it is translated as "household" in some English versions to emphasize the aspect of a people living with their God. Also in this verse the house is referred to as "the church of the living God"; it is the congregation of those who have been called out by the one true God to be together for Him. As such, as this Scripture shows, it has a testimony on the Earth to God's truth and to a standard of godly conduct.

We can see from these references that the house of God is where God, through His Spirit, desires to live among a people who are His own and who are living holy lives for Him.

The house as a building

The second way that the house of God is characterized in the epistles is as a structure. Unlike Old Testament times, it is not a physical structure; it is spiritual in character, made of living stones, people made alive spiritually. But the use of a building structure is a helpful metaphor for us. As we saw earlier, Peter describes how the house is continually being built up: *"Coming to Him as to a living stone which has been rejected by men, but is choice and precious in the sight of God, you also, as living stones, are being built up as a spiritual house for a holy priesthood, to offer up spiritual sacrifices acceptable to God through Jesus Christ"* (1 Peter 2:4,5).

It is as believers, desiring to grow up (mature) in their salvation, come to the Lord Jesus to be part of the house that God is building, and then continue to do so faithfully, that the house is built up and can function as a holy priesthood to God through Christ. Paul spoke to the Ephesians about this same building activity: *"You are no longer strangers and aliens, but you are fellow citizens with the saints, and are of God's household, having been built on the foundation of the apostles and prophets, Christ Jesus Himself being the corner stone, in whom the whole building, being fitted together, is growing into a holy temple in the Lord, in whom you also are being built together into a dwelling of God in the Spirit"* (Ephesians 2:19–22).

These saints in Ephesus had been brought into this position by being established on what they had been taught by the apostles and New Testament prophets, and they were being continually built together to be God's dwelling place.

Thirdly, Hebrews describes the house as what God is building today: *"Every house is built by someone, but the builder of all things is God. Now Moses was faithful in all His house as a servant, for a testimony of those things which were to be spoken later; but Christ was faithful as a Son over His house - whose house we are, if we hold fast our confidence and the boast of our hope firm until the end"* (Hebrews 3:4–6). The house that God is building today belongs to Christ; He is not just a servant in it but the Son over it, with all authority.

What is the house?

The picture that emerges from all this is not one in which all believers individually, or even the whole Body of Christ, are necessarily in the spiritual house of God today. Rather, the house of God consists of those faithful believers who have come to the Lord to function as His house for this purpose, who are living holy lives, and who appreciate and faithfully engage unitedly in the holy priesthood service of the house, as we will explore in the following chapters.

Stones

This metaphor that Peter used of living stones is in contrast to the "dead" inanimate stones that were used in building Solomon's temple and the others that followed it. Stones used in building work have always had a particular significance in Scripture, again beginning with Jacob at Bethel. Jacob took the single stone that he had used as a pillow and set it up as a pillar, a landmark of testimony. While it may not have indicated anything extraordinary to other people, it did testify that one person had been there for whom it had had some significance. It also showed Jacob where to return to and settle down after his time away.

Years later, when Joshua led the people across the Jordan into their promised land, he took twelve stones out of the river and set them up in a pile on the riverbank. These stones represented the twelve tribes of Israel. Again this was a landmark, a collective testimony to Israel's experience in that place. It (and several others like it) was used as a memorial for future generations. Large stones were used to build Solomon's great temple. They were cut out from a quarry under the city of Jerusalem. They were brought to the surface and shaped before being transported to the building site and placed in the wall of the temple: *The house, while it was being built, was built of stone prepared at the quarry, and there was neither hammer nor axe nor any iron tool heard in the house while it was being built"* (1 Kings 6:7)

.

In addition to building stones, Scripture also refers in various places to "precious stones," such as were used to adorn the temple that Solomon built (2 Chronicles 3:6). These were dressed stones which were well-fitting and finished. Precious stones will also adorn the future city of Jerusalem (Revelation 21:19). The apostle Paul told the saints in the church of God in Corinth that he had laid the foundation teaching in that place, but they were each to build on it with their works of service, which would be evaluated one day. He likened those works to either gold, silver, and precious stones, or else to worthless wood, hay, and stubble, which would be burnt up in the fire (1 Corinthians 3:10-15).

The foundation teaching of Christ (*"the apostles' teaching"* Acts 2:42), has been entirely laid down for us and we ourselves are intended to be the stones making up the house. It is then up to each of those who are in the house to be building it up (edifying it) by authentic spiritual service. How they do that will determine whether they "adorn" the teaching so that it is attractive to others: *"Showing all good faith so that they will adorn the doctrine of God our Savior in every respect"* (Titus 2:10). Thus disciples themselves as living stones are intended to form the house, while their service in it can beautify it.

Christ both a stone and a rock

There is a difference between the "rock" that Christ referred to in connection with the church that is His Body and the "stone" that is the foundation of the spiritual house in heaven:

- *"Upon this rock I will build My church"* (Matthew 16:18).
- *"Behold, I lay in Zion a choice stone, a precious corner stone"* (1 Peter 2:6).

As in the Old Testament, so in the New Testament, different words are used for "rock" and "stone," and they have very different meanings. A stone is moveable; a rock is not. In fact, the only time they occur together is in the expression "*a stone of stumbling and a rock of offense*" (Isaiah 8:14; Romans 9:33; 1 Peter 2:8 NKJV), in which they both refer to Christ.

Christ Himself is spoken of symbolically as a stone in several places. He is the stone "*cut out without hands*" referred to in Daniel 2:34 that would strike and crush the image representing the four Gentile super-powers. He is also, as we have just seen, "*the stone which the builders rejected*" (1 Peter 2:7), referring to the refusal of the Jewish leaders to accept Him. He is described as the "*living stone... a choice stone, a precious corner stone*" (1 Peter 2:4,6) that God has laid in heaven as the foundation of His spiritual house. The Jewish leaders were confounded by the fact that Jesus was God's choice to be the heir of His kingdom, as He spoke about in the parable of the landowner and the vine-dressers (Matthew 21:33–43). They could not accept that this one was the centrepiece of what God was building.

But this symbolism of Christ as a stone in His exaltation as a man in heaven is different imagery altogether from Him being referred to as the "rock." For example, David said in 2 Samuel 22:2: "*The LORD is my rock and my fortress and my deliverer.*" He was referring to God being eternal and unshakeable. Christ is explicitly referred to as the rock that followed the Israelites through the wilderness and provided water for them: "*They were drinking from a spiritual rock which followed them; and the rock was Christ*" (1 Corinthians 10:4). It was a symbol that reflected His deity.

The Jewish leaders were offended by the claim that Jesus was God's Son. They considered it to be "blasphemy." And that was the basis on which the Sanhedrin Council gave Him the death sentence (Matthew 26:63–65) and sent Him to Pilate to have it carried out. When Peter confessed to Christ that He was *the Christ, the Son of the living God*" (Matthew 16:16), he was confessing Christ's eternal and unchangeable deity. And Christ responded by saying, "*Upon this rock I will build My church; and the gates of Hades will not overpower it*" (verse 18). The rock of Christ's deity as God the Son is the basis for the church that is His Body. It is an eternal unshakeable truth, distinct from Him being placed after His resurrection and ascension as the *"chief corner stone"* of God's spiritual house. Christ's deity did not depend on His successful lifework, but His position in heaven today does. He always has been the "rock," but He has also become the "stone."

But how does this spiritual house actually work? How does it function as a "holy priesthood"? Who are the priests and why are priests needed for worshipping God? Finding answers to these questions is the next step in our journey.

CHAPTER SIX: THE HIGH PRIEST OF THE HOUSE OF GOD

"Since we have a great priest over the house of God..." (Hebrews 10:21)

Because the house of God is being built up to serve as a holy priesthood (1 Peter 2:5) it needs a high priest. A high priest is of necessity a man (Hebrews 5:1), and he acts as an intermediary between God and His people. He represents God to them and them to God, and makes their service acceptable. Further, to be the high priest, the person must be qualified and appointed by God Himself. Israel had a succession of them, beginning with Aaron (Exodus 28:1) and continuing with his descendants. Who then is the high priest of this new spiritual house, and what does he do?

God's oath

Is there anything that is sufficiently important to cause God to swear an oath? Yes, there is. When Christ ascended to heaven after He had completed His work on Earth, He was appointed to the post of high priest by God not only saying it (*"You are a priest forever according to the order of Melchizedek."* Hebrews 5:6) but also by Him swearing to it with an oath. His word and His oath are two things that are unchangeable (Hebrews 6:18). It was a permanent appointment. God's double assertion shows how important the appointment of the Lord Jesus as high priest is, since only He (who is both God and man) is ideally qualified.

A high priest under the old covenant could only serve during his lifetime, after which the responsibility passed on to his eldest son. In contrast, Christ has been established forever as high priest over God's house. There will never be another one. His position as high priest will never end, He cannot fail in it, and He will never be replaced. Even in the future temple in Christ's thousand-year reign on the Earth, and after that on the new eternal Earth, He will be the high priest of people's service to God. And so the privilege we have today of access to God and service through Christ is established forever.

Christ's service in the holy place

When Christ lived here as a man, He came to be a servant. He was "the servant of Jehovah" (Isaiah 42:1). He said, *"The Son of Man did not come to be served, but to serve, and to give His life a ransom for many"* (Mark 10:45). This earthly "ministry" to others uses the Greek word *"diakoneo"* in the original text, from which we get the word "deacon," referring to a person engaged in serving others. Christ was, literally, a deacon on Earth. He was sent from heaven as God's apostle to proclaim God to men so that He could then go back into heaven on their behalf (Hebrews 3:1).

Christ is now in heaven. Hebrews 9:24 tells us that Christ, after His completed sacrifice at Calvary, went into *"heaven itself,"* above all the created heavens, into the actual presence of God.

He is there now. He has gone in as a man, as Jesus the mediator of the new and better covenant. He went in as our forerunner (Hebrews 6:20) so that we would follow Him in, and He continues there as a minister in that sanctuary on our behalf: *"Christ did not enter a holy place made with hands, a mere copy of the true one, but into heaven itself, now to appear in the presence of God for us"* (Hebrews 9:24).

In that place, He is *"a minister in the sanctuary"* (Hebrews 8:2). That "ministry" is the exalted ministry of divine service (Greek: *"leitourgos"*). It is a very different kind of service than His earthly ministry, but He is still serving. His ministry, when contrasted with the service of the Old Testament priests, is described as being *"more excellent"* (Hebrews 8:6). It is what makes possible the spiritual service of the holy priesthood, and what makes that service acceptable to God His Father, as 1 Peter 2:5 states. Coming in any other way would be unacceptable.

And so we as disciples today do not need a person on Earth to take us to God in worship. Christ has been exalted in heaven to do that for us. Thus Christ, who is both God and man, is the only way to God (John 14:6), both in salvation and in service.

Our role as priests

The priests in Israel carried out many services in connection with the house of God. They offered on the altar the animal sacrifices that people brought, and they maintained the lamp stand, the table, and the incense in the holy place. In addition, the high priest represented the people as a whole before God, such as on the Day of Atonement, when he alone could go into the most holy place to make atonement for them. Without the high priest, the other priests could not have functioned. So it is with us today as a priesthood – we need our high priest.

But He also needs us. Just as the high priest of Israel needed to receive offerings from the people in order to present them to God on their behalf, so does Christ today: *"For every high priest is appointed to offer both gifts and sacrifices; so it is necessary that this high priest also have something to offer"* (Hebrews 8:3). The house of God cannot function without worshippers who offer. Christ takes our offerings, perfects them, and offers them on our behalf to God. The role of the holy priesthood, then, is to bring spiritual sacrifices and offer them to God through Christ.

What is particular about priestly service?

Offering spiritual sacrifices as a holy priesthood has a number of distinctive characteristics, such as the following:

- The worship is directed to God the Father, and not to Christ or to the Holy Spirit. (*"He has made us to be a kingdom, priests to His God and Father"* Revelation 1:6). We will see in a later chapter what is particularly significant about addressing our worship to "His God and Father."

- Christ's part in this worship is not to receive it for Himself, but to offer it to God on our behalf as high priest, as a man mediating in the presence of God. His part is what makes it acceptable. (*"Through Him then, let us continually offer up a sacrifice of praise to*

God" Hebrews 13:15; "... *a holy priesthood, to offer up spiritual sacrifices acceptable to God through Jesus Christ"* 1 Peter 2:5).

- The worship is offered by a collective people, not just an aggregation of individuals. They have a distinct identity as the people of God, the holy priesthood. Holy priesthood service is by a united people, who worship as one. Those whom Peter had described as a holy priesthood, he also described as follows: *"You are a chosen race, a royal priesthood, a holy nation, a people for God's own possession"* (1 Peter 2:9).

The apostle Paul also referred to this collective worship in writing to the church in Rome when he said to them, *"Be of the same mind with one another according to Christ Jesus, so that with one accord you may with one voice glorify the God and Father of our Lord Jesus Christ"* (Romans 15:5,6). This service of the collective priesthood is in addition to and quite distinct from our personal communion with God the Father and with the Lord Jesus, which each believer can enjoy individually by the Holy Spirit: *"Our fellowship is with the Father, and with His Son Jesus Christ"* (1 John 1:3).

A kingdom of priests

Not only were these disciples to whom Peter was writing part of the *"holy priesthood"* (in other words, a people totally devoted to divine service in the worship of God), but they were also described as a *"royal priesthood"* (1 Peter 2:9). This expression is actually the same as was applied to Israel, at

Mount Sinai, when they were receiving the covenant from God and were told that they would be a "kingdom of priests" (Exodus 19:6).

There is an integral connection between disciples who are the spiritual house of God today (1 Peter 2:5) and those who are God's kingdom today (verse 9). Peter applied the different terms to the same people. The kingdom of God refers to those who are united under God and the authority of the Lord Jesus, serving Him together according to His commandments. A great deal of what is written in the New Testament is about how the kingdom of God is to function. That was the subject matter of the Lord's instructions to His apostles during His last forty days with them (Acts 1:3). Just as Israel was God's kingdom on Earth in the past and had God's house among them, so God's house and His kingdom are linked today.

We may sometimes hear or read the expression "the priesthood of all believers"—meaning that all believers in Christ are priests. This is too inaccurate an expression. All believers, by virtue of the new birth, have a birth-right to priesthood, but all do not exercize that birthright. Serving as priests is a collective activity. It is the work of a priest*hood*. It is therefore necessary to become part of the priesthood in order to carry out that service (just as an athlete needs to become part of a team in order to engage in a team sport). We sometimes refer to people "going into the priesthood" as a chosen vocation, to receive training and ordination as priests in a church. But, as 1 Peter 2:5 and Revelation 1:6 show, becoming part of this holy and royal priesthood takes place when a disciple unites with other disciples as part of the kingdom and house of God.

A living stone that is not built into the spiritual house does not fulfill its intended purpose, just as a priest who is not operating as part of the priesthood is not fulfilling his purpose. However, when disciples today do become part of the spiritual house of God, and therefore part of the holy priesthood, how do they go about offering their spiritual sacrifices? To answer this question, we need to look next at the subject of worship in the house.

CHAPTER SEVEN: THE WORSHIP OF THE HOUSE OF GOD

"A spiritual house for a holy priesthood, to offer up spiritual sacrifices acceptable to God through Jesus Christ." (1 Peter 2:5)

Worship is the primary purpose of the house of God. As we have seen, there is a high priest in place to enable this to occur. But where does it take place? Perhaps we may assume that when we gather together here on Earth for worship, Christ comes down to join us where we are. We may base this, for example, on Matthew 18:20: *"For where two or three have gathered together in My name, I am there in their midst."* But as the context of that verse shows, this is not referring to worship at all, but to decision-making and judgment in the church. And so we have to look elsewhere for the answer to our question.

Christ is in heaven

We know that Christ has been exalted to the right hand of the throne of God, and has been told by His Father to remain there: *"Sit at My right hand until I make Your enemies a footstool for your feet"* (Hebrews 1:13). And so Christ does not leave heaven. In fact, as He promised, the next time He will do so will be to receive us to Himself and take us bodily back with Him to enjoy His presence for ever.

Christ went into heaven as a "forerunner" (Hebrews 6:20), to pave the way for us to go there in worship, and He is now there on our behalf: *"Christ did not enter a holy place made with hands, a mere copy of the true one, but into heaven itself, now to appear in the presence of God for us"* (Hebrews 9:24). If Christ our high priest is in heaven and we are on Earth, how can we offer our spiritual sacrifices to God through Him? Christ does not have to come down here to receive them. It is the Holy Spirit, who is within us, that enables our worship of God in heaven: *"We... worship in the Spirit of God"* (Philippians 3:3). This is distinct from the individual communion that He brings about (2 Corinthians 13:14).

The Holy Spirit has been sent to us on Earth for exactly this purpose, to effect the presence of Christ in His absence (John 14:16; 15:26; 16:14). That is why, for example, the church in Ephesus was told that they were *"a dwelling of God in the Spirit"* (Ephesians 2:22). It has always been the work of the Spirit to bring about on Earth what God is doing from heaven.

Because God is spirit and desires to be worshipped *"in spirit and truth"* (John 4:24), the Holy Spirit enables us in our spiritual faculties to offer our sacrifices to God in heaven itself. Christ does not come down to us when we worship; we draw near to Him in spirit. It is the Holy Spirit who makes it possible for those of us who are living on the Earth to worship God the Father who is in heaven. Ephesians 2:18 shows how each member of the trinity is involved in such activity: *"through Him* [that is, Christ Jesus] *we both have our access in one Spirit to the Father."*

Not only is Christ in heaven now, He is in the heavenly sanctuary, serving as high priest. Thus, if Christ remains in heaven, and our worship is offered through Him, then it must take place there, not here on the Earth. As He has already gone there, so we also can now enter the holy place: *"Therefore, brethren, since we have confidence to enter the holy place by the blood of Jesus..."* (Hebrews 10:19).

Where do we come?

The men of Israel came for worship to the temple on Mount Zion in Jerusalem. Today we have: *"...come to Mount Zion and to the city of the living God, the heavenly Jerusalem, and to myriads of angels, to the general assembly and church of the firstborn who are enrolled in heaven, and to God, the Judge of all, and to the spirits of the righteous made perfect, and to Jesus, the mediator of a new covenant, and to the sprinkled blood, which speaks better than the blood of Abel"* (Hebrews 12:22–24).

After leaving Egypt, Israel had to travel for many years to reach the place where God wished them to worship Him. He brought them into the land of their inheritance (Canaan). Correspondingly we have come to a "better country," to heaven (Hebrews 11:16). Within that country, Israel came to the designated mountain of Zion; we have come to the mountain of God in heaven (the heavenly Mount Zion). Then on that mountain Israel came to the holy city of Jerusalem; we have come to the city of the living God, the heavenly Jerusalem. Finally, in that city Israel came to the temple, the house of God. But they could only enter its gates and come into its courts (Psalm 100:4); they were barred from the innermost sanctuary by the command of the Lord (Hebrews 9:8). But we have come to the holy place of the sanctuary of God's throne where God is, together with Jesus our mediator. God has called us into His own immediate presence in heaven, to worship Him in spirit and truth. The worship of the holy priesthood takes place in heaven, in the presence of God, where Christ has gone and is today. There is no higher place.

This is an amazing truth. Christ is now in the presence of God as a man, as mediator of the new covenant. That covenant is eternal and is based on His blood having been poured out in death at Calvary and sprinkled (figuratively), that is applied, in heaven (Hebrews 9:23; compare Leviticus 16:14). He is the "great priest" (Hebrews 10:19) over the house of God, and so those in that house are not only allowed to come in, but are summoned to come in by God Himself. It would be wrong for us to refuse that call, or to "shrink back," as Hebrews 10:39 tells us. As a result, we have the strong exhortation: *"Let us draw near"* (Hebrews 10:22).

The way in

So much of the teaching of the book of Hebrews uses contrasts between the old order of Israel's service with the service of God today. These include the covenant at Sinai, the law, the tabernacle service, and the priestly roles of Aaron and his sons. Even though the tabernacle was only a replica (a *"shadow"* Hebrews 8:5) of the true sanctuary in heaven where we are enabled to worship today, access to its most holy place was restricted, except for the high priest. He was required to go in alone on the annual Day of Atonement in the tenth month.

Apart from that annual occasion, the most holy place was hidden to the outside observer: *"The Holy Spirit is signifying this, that the way into the holy place has not yet been disclosed while the outer tabernacle is still standing"* (Hebrews 9:8). The veil separated the holy place from the rest of the tabernacle or temple and kept it hidden. It was also the first covering of the Ark of the covenant and the mercy seat when they were carried in the wilderness; the people never saw them.

In contrast, the people of God today have access through the veil, which is the present living body of Jesus Christ: *"Therefore, brethren, since we have confidence to enter the holy place by the blood of Jesus, by a new and living way which He inaugurated for us through the veil, that is, His flesh"* (Hebrews 10:19,20). The fact that there is a perfect man in God's immediate presence who is there on our behalf, and who has cleansed all our sin by shedding His blood, is what permits us also to go in now in spirit.

So...let us draw near

Chapters 10 and 12 of Hebrews are the summit of the epistle. They describe the thrilling privilege of the collective access that God's people have now into His actual sanctuary in heaven. The previous chapters led up to this. The writer knew that it was vital for these early disciples to realize that this privilege had been made available to them, so that they could take advantage of it *"in full assurance of faith"* (10:22). It is just as vital that we realize it.

This is why chapter 11 is inserted, to present that great catalogue of faithful ones, the "*cloud of witnesses*" from the past (Hebrews 12:1), to urge us to have full assurance of faith, to draw near together in full confidence, and not to hold back. None of them had the prospect that we now have, and yet they were so faithful to what they were given, even to the point of death in some cases. This chapter 11 is encouraging not just our personal lives of faith but especially, as the context shows, our "*full assurance of faith*" (Hebrews 10:22) in united divine service as the people of God. Faith on our part makes us grasp that our worship in the holy place in heaven is real even though we cannot see it physically.

The first part of chapter 12 also amplifies this experience. It describes God's disciplinary process with us as His sons, so that we might share in His holiness and so avoid the danger of us shrinking back, which we are warned about in Hebrews 10:26-39. Verse 18 then resumes the portrayal of the worship of God's house by describing where we have come and who are there. It describes the great congregation in heaven itself, including countless numbers of angels, believers who died in faith in Old Testament times, and members of the Body of Christ who have died. They are all focussed on God on His throne and on Jesus the mediator who has made it all possible. This is the company that we as the holy priesthood are with spiritually when we worship. This is worship in spirit and truth.

If this describes the tremendous privilege now offered to us as disciples of the Lord Jesus Christ, we need to determine who exactly can take advantage of it, and what conditions they must meet so that they can be sure that they are included.

Who for example was Peter referring to when he said, "*You are being built up as a spiritual house?*" (1 Peter 2:5) Who was the book of Hebrews written to, urging them to "*draw near?*" (Hebrews 10:22) What is required of believers in order to have this privilege? For the answers to this question, we need to go back to the third chapter of this epistle to the Hebrews.

CHAPTER EIGHT: THE BIG "IF"

"Whose house we are, if we hold fast our confidence and the boast of our hope firm until the end." (Hebrews 3:6)

Aaron was the first high priest of Israel, but Moses was the one charged with building the tabernacle. It was he who received the precise instructions on Mount Sinai, and he was told that it was essential that it be built exactly as it was shown to him. Moses followed the directions precisely, and so he is described in the New Testament as a faithful servant: *"Moses was faithful in all His house as a servant, for a testimony of those things which were to be spoken later"* (Hebrews 3:5). Because the faithful Moses carefully followed the instructions, we have today an incomparable teaching tool to aid our service.

It is all about faithfulness

In Hebrews 3:1–6, however, it is Christ's faithfulness in God's house that is especially highlighted: *"Consider Jesus, the Apostle and High Priest of our confession; He was faithful to Him who appointed Him, as Moses also was in all His house. For He has been counted worthy of more glory than Moses, by just so much as the builder of the house has more honor than the house"* (Hebrews 3:1-3).

Although Christ serves in the heavenly sanctuary today, His position is vastly different from that of Moses. He is not a servant, but the Son over the house of God: *"Moses was faithful in all His house as a servant, for a testimony of those things which were to be spoken later; but Christ...as a Son over His house"* (Hebrews 3:5,6).

There is a big difference in status between a son and a servant in a household. The firstborn son was the heir; he was treated as the future head of the household. He had permanent status and rank in the house, whereas the servant was required to follow orders and could be discharged at any time. The servant's word did not carry any authority unless he was expressly speaking on behalf of the master of the house or his son. (We get an illustration of this in the Lord's story of the prodigal son in Luke chapter 15. After the son returned home, he was willing to become just a servant in the house. He knew the difference.)

The exaltation of Christ by his Father in giving Him all authority in heaven and on Earth (Matthew 28:18) included making Him Son over His house. He is its chief corner stone. He is the one who is first, against whom all others are measured and lined up, which tells us of His pre-eminence and authority. Included in that authority is serving as its high priest: *"Since we have a great priest over the house of God ..."* (Hebrews 10:21). As typified by Melchizedek, He is both king and priest (Hebrews 6:20; 7:1; Genesis 14:18).

God is the builder of the spiritual house today and He does it through Christ (Hebrews 3:1-6). Since more honour is due to the builder than to what he builds, Christ is worthy of more honour than the living stones who make up the house.

The condition

In addition to Moses and the Lord Jesus, Hebrews 3:1-6 refers to a third class of persons, today's disciples, who must show the same characteristic of faithfulness. The passage introduces a condition when it says, *"if we hold fast ..."* (In the Greek text the word for "if" makes it clear that it is a condition - "if indeed".) This condition of faithfulness is that *"we hold fast our confidence and the boast of our hope firm until the end."*

This holding fast has nothing to do with us maintaining our salvation; that is totally out of our hands (John 10:28). Our hope in Christ for eternity is secure, and we have been given the Holy Spirit as its guarantee (2 Corinthians 5:5; Ephesians 1:13). Nor does it imply that those to whom the epistle was written were just nominal Christians who needed to become true believers. Instead this holding fast is about disciples of the Lord Jesus continuing to believe in this "hope."

What is our "hope"?

We tend to think of a hope as being something uncertain in the future, something that we are wishing for and looking forward to. And so when Hebrews 3:6 talks about us holding fast to our confidence and glorying in that hope, we might assume that it is referring to the future hope that Christians have of Christ coming from heaven for them. That is the hope that is referred to, for example, in Titus 2:13: *"Looking for the blessed hope and the appearing of the glory of our great God and Savior, Christ Jesus"*. If that were what it was referring to, then a believer could belong to God's house only as long as he or she believed and looked forward to Christ's return.

But a hope can also be something we want now (such as, "I hope I am making myself clear in this book"). Hebrews 3:6 is referring to such a present hope, not one that we have to wait for, as these verses explain:

"This hope we have as an anchor of the soul, a hope both sure and steadfast and one which enters within the veil, where Jesus has entered as a forerunner for us" (Hebrews 6:19,20).

"...bringing in of a better hope, through which we draw near to God" (Hebrews 7:19).

This hope is the reality of Christ in the presence of God as priest on behalf of God's people, permitting them to draw near. Both of these verses are in the present tense; the entering and drawing near is now. It is a *"better hope"* than Israel ever enjoyed under the law. We are to *"take hold"* of this hope (Hebrews 6:18), and then to *"hold fast"* our confession of it (Hebrews 10:23).

In the Bible the word "hope" does not imply any uncertainty or something we may just wish for. Rather it is something invisible that we are longing for, whether in the future or now. What gives us assurance about its fulfilment is our faith: *"Faith is the assurance of things hoped for, the conviction of things not seen"* (Hebrews 11:1). Both hope and faith are stated in Hebrews chapter 10 as being critical elements in our spiritual access to God in worship: *"Let us draw near with a sincere heart in full assurance of faith"* (Hebrews 10:22); and *"Let us hold fast the confession of our hope without wavering"* (Hebrews 10:23). We have been given the hope; by faith we need to avail ourselves of it.

What is our confession?

Our worship to God involves us making confession (the Greek word is *homologeo*, meaning what we acknowledge and profess) to His name. We are able to do this because we hold fast the confession of our hope, we believe and acknowledge the truth of God that has been given to us through Christ. Christ is referred to as the apostle and high priest of our confession: *"Consider Jesus, the Apostle and High Priest of our confession"* (Hebrews 3:1). As its apostle He was sent out by God to bring God's Word to us; as its high priest He has gone back in to God to serve as high priest on behalf of the people of God, who hold and keep that Word. By holding fast by faith to this confession, we are enabled to draw near into the presence of God.

One of the results of this is that we can draw near in spirit to God's throne to express ourselves to Him in prayer: *"...we have a great high priest who has passed through the heavens, Jesus the Son of God, let us hold fast our confession...therefore let us draw near with confidence to the throne of grace..."* (Hebrews 4:14,16). Another is that we can draw near in worship, by entering into the holy place (Hebrews 10:19-25). This involves us offering a sacrifice of praise pertaining to this confession: *"Through Jesus, therefore, let us continually offer to God a sacrifice of praise - the fruit of lips that confess his name"* (Hebrews 13:15 NIV).

The Greek words for *"confess His name"* (NIV) are sometimes translated as *"give/giving thanks to His name"* (NASB, NKJV) and sometimes as *"make confession to His name"* (American Standard Version, English Revised Version).

What does it all mean?

Our participation in the house of God is therefore a conditional matter. It is conditional on our faithfulness in holding fast to our confidence in and glorying of our hope, whereby we continually draw near with a sincere heart as the people of God to worship Him together in spirit and truth through Jesus Christ our high priest, confessing God's name (and worth) to Him. As we hold fast we are able to continue in the house. If we willfully disregard it or neglect it, our place in the house will be in jeopardy.

The "pillar and support of the truth"

Paul is another writer who mentioned the conditions of being the house of God. When he was giving instructions to the young man Timothy about elders and deacons in churches of God, he described the house as "the pillar and support of the truth": *"I write so that you will know how one ought to conduct himself in the household of God, which is the church of the living God, the pillar and support of the truth"* (1 Timothy 3:15).

The Greek word used here is *'oikos,'* translated "household" in NASB and NIV and translated "house" in NKJV and King James Version. It is referring to the house of God. Paul's description of the house of God as *"the pillar and support of the truth"* means that it must stand for and remain faithful to the truth of God. Otherwise, those in it cannot continue to be God's house. The condition of holding fast the confession of our hope, that we have just been considering, is therefore an aspect of a more comprehensive condition of holding fast to the truth of God. This means that if error or division comes in among the people of God with respect to the Lord's teaching, their position as God's house is at risk. This is exactly what happened after the first century, when the apostles had passed on. Waves of wrong teaching came into the churches, as we looked at in chapter 2. God's truth was no longer being testified to and upheld. Exactly when God stopped recognizing them as His house we do not know, but it was not the first time it had happened. God had vacated His house before, as Christ had announced when He was in Jerusalem (Matthew 23:38).

What is "the truth"?

What then is "the truth" that is being referred to in 1 Timothy 3:15 that must be upheld? In the previous chapter, Paul had told Timothy that God *"desires all men to be saved and to come to the knowledge of the truth"* (1 Timothy 2:4). In his second epistle to Timothy, he referred to people who were *"always learning and never able to come to the knowledge of the truth"* (2 Timothy 3:7). And so this topic of "the truth" was a recurring theme of Paul's to Timothy. It referred to the whole body of teaching for disciples in that day (and today), and is also referred to also as "the faith" (see Appendix B). It is the whole gospel and counsel of God that apply to men and women today (Acts 20:27). It includes not only how to be eternally saved, but also how believers are to live, and how they are to worship and serve God. It is comprehensive.

When Paul said that the house of God must be its "pillar and support," he was saying that it must be a place of obedience to all the teaching of the Lord. Since the house of God is where God Himself lives and is served, it must also be a place of godly conduct and proper order. Doctrine (teaching) and related practice is thus an essential element of being the house of God today. Yet what we see today in the Christian world is a huge diversity of doctrine and practice.

CHAPTER NINE: GROWING INTO A HOLY TEMPLE

"In whom the whole building, being fitted together, is growing into a holy temple in the Lord..." (Ephesians 2:21)

The many Gentile saints in the church at Ephesus in Asia Minor did not have the same background as their Jewish counterparts. They did not have the same knowledge of the Old Testament nor the heritage of divine service from their ancestors. Most had been pagans, and the service of God was new to them. So the apostle Paul, whose special mission was to these Gentiles, assured them that they had been given all the same privileges as their Jewish Christian colleagues.

Full rights and privileges

In the second chapter of Ephesians, he reviewed for them their spiritual experience to that point. He reminded them of the state that they had been in before they came to Christ: *"dead in your trespasses and sins"* (verse 1) ... *"having no hope and without God in the world"* (verse 12). But then everything had changed: *"by grace you have been saved through faith* (verse 8). He said *"remember that you were at that time separate from Christ, excluded from the commonwealth of Israel, and strangers to the covenants of promise"* (verse 12). But now they no longer had an inferior status:

"So then you are no longer strangers and aliens, but you are fellow citizens with the saints, and are of God's household, having been built on the foundation of the apostles and prophets, Christ

Jesus Himself being the corner stone, in whom the whole building, being fitted together, is growing into a holy temple in the Lord, in whom you also are being built together into a dwelling of God in the Spirit" (verses 19-22).

Laying the foundation

Paul describes in these verses the structure and formation of that spiritual house that they were part of, the same house that we have been looking at, as referred to in 1 Timothy 3:15 and 1 Peter 2:5, and the epistle to the Hebrews. God has only one spiritual house for believers today. The apostle outlined that it began with Christ Jesus being laid by God His Father as the corner stone in heaven after His ascension, as 1 Peter 2:6 also describes. Then, corresponding to that foundation, the apostles together with New Testament prophets laid the foundation teaching as they established churches of disciples in various places in their travels. That consistent teaching was what the Lord Jesus had commanded the eleven before his ascension when He spent the forty days with them *"speaking of the things concerning the kingdom of God"* (Acts 1:3), and additionally revealed to Paul (Galatians 1:12–17; 1 Corinthians 11:23).

Each church (collection of saints) that was established on this foundation teaching in each locality was what God was building in that place. Paul used the same language when he referred to the church in Corinth as *"God's building"* (1 Corinthians 3:9). (Paul did not include himself by saying "we," as he did earlier in that verse when referring to working with them for God, because he was not in the church in Corinth that he was writing to. Each church was described spiritually as a building. Together they formed the temple of God.)

How many buildings?

Ephesians 2:21 in our English Bible translations can be confusing. This verse is often translated *"in whom the whole building, being fitted together, is growing into a holy temple in the Lord."* The word for "whole" is the Greek word *"pas,"* which is used frequently in the New Testament. When it is used without the article, as here, it means "every", not "the whole". Rather than this verse being translated *"the whole building,"* it is better read as *"every building"* (or, as some versions have it, *"each several building")*. (To illustrate this meaning of the Greek word *"pas,"* consider two other examples where it is used: (1) 1 Corinthians 11:3: *"Christ is the head of every man"*; this clearly does not mean *"the head of the whole man"*; and (2) Ephesians 5:20 *"always giving thanks for all things..."*; clearly again this does not mean *"giving thanks for the whole thing."*)

Thus Ephesians 2:21,22 may be read (and interpreted) as: *"in whom every building* [that is, each local church], *being fitted* [joined] *together, is growing into* [the] *holy temple* [God's house] *in the Lord, in whom you also* [the church in Ephesus] *are being built together into a dwelling of God in the Spirit."* (One reason why this distinction between singular and plural is important here is that it can help us to avoid assuming that *"the whole building"* is referring to the Body of Christ.)

What Paul is describing here is each local church being established on the same foundation teaching of the apostles (and New Testament prophets), and being united to all other such churches, resulting in them all growing as the temple (house) of God on Earth. He then particularized it to the church in Ephesus, telling them that they also were part of it. They were a habitation (literally it means "a settled dwelling place" - Greek: *kat-oikeo*.) of God in the Spirit. In other words, God was living among them collectively in the person of the Holy Spirit; they were part of the total house.

This picture of many individual buildings (local churches) constituting one house is similar to the composition of the temple that existed in the Lord's time: *"Jesus came out from the temple and was going away when His disciples came up to point out the temple buildings to Him. And He said to them, 'Do you not see all these things? Truly I say to you, not one stone here will be left upon another, which will not be torn down'"* (Matthew 24:1,2). That temple had multiple buildings also. Peter does not mention the individual constituent buildings in his description of the living stones in 1 Peter 2:5; he was not writing to an individual church in that case, but to saints in various areas.

How the house is built up

In summary then, we can see that:

- Christ in His exaltation has been placed by God in heaven as the chief corner stone of the spiritual house (1 Peter 2:6).

- Churches of disciples (who are referred to as "saints," Ephesians 1:1) are formed on Earth corresponding to that foundation in heaven, by adherence to the uniform teaching of the apostles.

- Individuals come to Christ for salvation, continue as obedient disciples, and come to be added together as living stones, being built into this house (1 Peter 2:5).

- The individual churches are united in teaching and practice with each other; this outcome of *"the unity of the faith"* is the goal set out for all members of the Body of Christ (Ephesians 4:13).

- Those churches together constitute the house (temple) of God on Earth, as God's dwelling place among His people (2 Corinthians 6:16).

- This house has the supreme privilege of united access into the presence of God in spirit, for the purpose of collectively offering spiritual service as a holy priesthood, through the ministry of Christ as high priest (Hebrews 10:19–23).

- If error is introduced and allowed to continue, or if those in the house fail to continue to give effect to their privilege of access in worship, they can no longer continue to be God's house (Hebrews 3:6). They cannot of course lose their eternal salvation in Christ, and they do not cease to be members of the Body of Christ.

This view of things is very different from what we get by assuming that all believers, by virtue solely of their membership in the Body of Christ, are in the house of God and have the privilege of collective worship as God's people. That assumption leaves out the essential requirements of adherence to the Lord's teaching, faithfulness in divine service, and unity. However the view that all members of the Body of Christ should be united in this way and have this privilege is very much the ideal that we should be striving for.

CHAPTER TEN: LINKING HEAVEN AND EARTH

"Behold, a ladder was set on the earth with its top reaching to heaven." (Genesis 28:12)

The house of God in Old Testament times was strictly earthly, though it was a *"shadow of the heavenly things"* (Hebrews 8:5). The spiritual house of God today has both heavenly and earthly aspects. The living stones, believers, that are joined to make up the house are on Earth. They are disciples gathered together in accordance with what the apostles taught, and they enjoy its privilege of divine service. Their audible expression of worship uses their physical voices. But their access is into heaven itself in spirit, where God is and where Jesus the Son of God continuously ministers as their high priest. It is spiritual service. This link between heaven and Earth is an essential element of the house of God. It is what Jacob was shown in the dream that he saw, as he realized that the house of God, where he was, was the gate of heaven (Genesis 28:17).

Lampstands on Earth and the sanctuary in heaven

The tabernacle that Israel constructed in the wilderness had two compartments: a "holy place" and a "most holy place." Inside the holy place was the golden lamp stand, the table of showbread and the golden altar of incense. In the most holy place was the Ark of the Covenant covered by the mercy seat, above which dwelt the immediate presence of God. Today there is no division into two sections. These items of furniture mostly speak of Christ who is in heaven; however the lampstand particularly speaks of testimony by saints on Earth today in local churches of God (Revelation 1:12).

Foundations in heaven and on Earth

God has placed Christ as the foundation stone of the spiritual house in the heavenly Mount Zion (1 Peter 2:6). Corresponding to this, the apostles laid on Earth the foundation teaching that they had received from Him, as they established churches in various places. If they had taught anything other than that in any place, the disciples in that place could not have been part of the house. Everywhere the apostles travelled, they established the same teaching, based directly on what the Lord Jesus had personally taught them. Even though the apostle Paul was not with the other apostles before the Lord's ascension, he also received the self-same teaching directly from the Lord (1 Corinthians 11:23; 15:8).

"According to the grace of God which was given to me, like a wise master builder I laid a foundation...no man can lay a foundation other than the one which is laid, which is Jesus Christ" (1 Corinthians 3:10,11). This matching of the foundation teaching on Earth with what God had done in heaven is a fulfillment of the Lord's words when he taught His disciples to pray: *"Your kingdom come; your will be done on earth as it is in heaven"* (Matthew 6:10). What takes place on Earth must correspond to what is true in heaven, for God to live among us.

Service by a collective people

It is important to note in all this that the service of the people of God was and is primarily collective. The individual's contribution is always vital, but God always desires unity. Unity is at the very essence of the person of God, three in one, joined in perfect harmony and love. It is the unity that is reflected in the single name into which disciples are baptized: *"the name of the Father and the Son and the Holy Spirit"* (Matthew 28:19). For example, God desires unity when He joins a man and a woman in marriage. Again this is a three-way unity of the two people with Himself, which is why today marriage by disciples should be *"in the Lord"* (1 Corinthians 7:39). He wants this same unity in the people that He calls out to serve Him.

For example, Israel was covenanted to be one holy nation for God. They were to be united both with Him and with each other in the two greatest commandments of their law: *"You shall love the Lord your God with all your heart, and with all your soul, and with all your mind...";* and *"You shall love your neighbour as yourself"* (Matthew 22:37,39). Similarly, when Moses was instructed to ratify the covenant that established Israel as God's unique people, His peculiar treasure (Exodus 19:6), he took blood and sprinkled both the book of the law and the people (Exodus 24:6-8; Hebrews 9:19,20). They thereby became jointly bound to Him by that covenant.

Although individuals in Israel brought offerings and engaged in certain activity, the focus was on the nation as one people - the particular individuals comprising it were secondary. For example, God had decreed that His people Israel would enter the promised land; that could not be denied. Yet certain persons failed to enter, due to their disobedience and lack of faith (Jude verse 5). But others took their place, and so God's promise was fulfilled collectively. They went in as a nation under Joshua's leadership.

In a similar way, the focus of the book of Hebrews is on the people of God and the privileges given to them. In it several specific warnings are given, including some to individuals which show that it is possible for any one person to miss out on the privileges that are made available to the people as a whole. For example:

"Take care, brethren, that there not be in any one of you an evil, unbelieving heart that falls away from the living God" (3:12).

"Therefore let us be diligent to enter that rest, so that no one will fall, through following the same example of disobedience" (4:11).

What God is looking for then is a united people who function together, with a single identity as one holy nation, one spiritual house, one priesthood. It is not merely an aggregation of individuals being in one place worshipping God, but a people drawing near as one. It is only by the work of the Spirit of God that this unity can be achieved in practice (Ephesians 4:3).

The Amen

This collective view of things helps us to understand the significance of saying *"the Amen"* (1 Corinthians 14:16) at the collective giving of thanks and prayer. When a church gathers to engage in this activity, several men may speak in turn, voicing the thanksgivings and prayers (1 Timothy 2:8). When they do this, they are not just speaking for themselves, but are representing the whole company. This is then acknowledged by all the others saying "Amen," meaning "so be it," and so associating themselves with what has been said.

Understanding this collective identity and functioning is a vital part of realizing the opportunity that is presented to us to be the people of God and the house of God today. How we gather on Earth in our service for God must reflect this unity and collective identity. How the Bible tells us that we are to gather in order to do this is the subject of our next section: Discovering God's Church.

CHAPTER ELEVEN: GOD'S HOUSE - A SUMMARY

The main points about God's house that have emerged in this book can be summarized as follows:

- God began to disclose His desire to live among His people on Earth in the book of Genesis.

- God's first house built by men on Earth was the tabernacle in the wilderness, given to His people Israel. It represented the true holy place in heaven.

- Today God's house is not only the result of the fact that the Holy Spirit indwells individual believers. It is God the Spirit living among a united people.
- The house today is spiritual. It consists of disciples being built together, on the foundational teaching of the apostles, to form local churches, which are united in that teaching and practice to constitute God's house.

- God's house is different from the Body of Christ in many ways, but principally because it requires on-going faithfulness to the truth of God to be in it.
- The house of God consists of people and is on Earth. God's presence here is in the person of the Holy Spirit. Through Him spiritual access is provided into the sanctuary in heaven, where are God the Father and Jesus Christ.

- The symbolism of Christ being a rock (representing His eternal deity, on which He is building the church which is His Body) is different from that of Him being exalted to be the stone chosen by God to be the foundation of the spiritual house of God.

- Christ is in heaven, serving as high priest over God's house. This is referred to as our hope. He presents the people's offerings to His God and Father and makes them acceptable.

- Holding fast to belief in this hope is central to the conditions for believers continuing to be God's house.

- Those in the house are urged to continually draw near into the sanctuary in heaven to offer their spiritual sacrifices through Christ.

- If these then are the prerequisites of being in God's house today, each of us as a disciple of the Lord Jesus should ask ourselves "Am I part of that house, or am I missing something"?

"Send forth your light and your truth,

let them guide me;

let them bring me to your holy mountain,

to the place where you dwell."

(Psalm 43:3 NIV)

Did you love *Discovering God's House*? Then you should read *Our Spiritual Journey*[1] by Keith Dorricott!

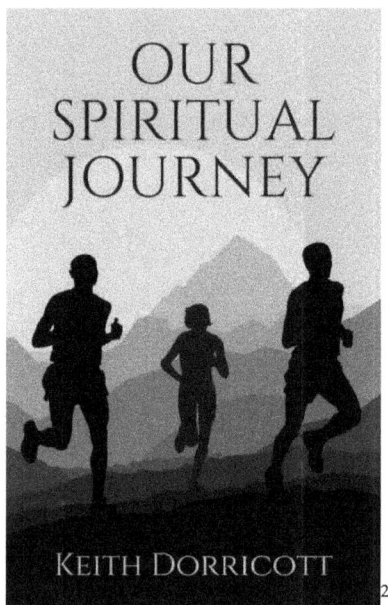

In this practical and Bible-based book, Keith Dorricott outlines a journey that God wants every Christian to embark upon, one that involves our own spirit and the Holy Spirit and that can result in a final destination of victorious Christian living!

1. The Journey of Spirituality
2. Understanding How God Made Us
3. From Before the Cradle to Beyond the Grave
4. Being Spiritual, Not Fleshly

---

1. https://books2read.com/u/ml5Wq9

2. https://books2read.com/u/ml5Wq9

Also by Keith Dorricott